I wish I knew

NOTES FROM A BREAST CANCER SURVIVOR

Fanny Barry

Blue Heron Book Works, LLC
Allentown, PA

Third edition Copyright © 2017 Fanny Barry
All rights reserved. No part of this book may be reproduced without the written permission of the author or the publisher

This book was originally published and copyrighted in 2005 in three parts:
I wish I Knew…I Wish I Knew How to Help….
I Wish I Knew Who I've Become.
They were subsequently republished in ebook form.

Cover image: Fanny Barry
Cover design by: Angie Zambrano
Front cover design and layout by: Fanny Barry & Megan M. Greene
ISBN: 978-0-9991460-2-6

Blue Heron Book Works, LLC
Allentown, PA 18104
www.blueheronbookworks.com

Thanks to my publisher, Blue Heron Bookworks and Bathsheba Monk for being the muse behind these wonderful pieces of inspirational art. I still remember when I showed her the draft nervously, holding a hand to my bald head. When she said, "Fanny, these are really beautiful." I started to cry and started the journey to publish and illustrate them. She never lost faith in them or me.
Also thanks to her wonderful husband who as the ultimate critic gave me faith that these books were in fact good.

And thanks to graphic designer extraordinaire, Megan Greene, also my cousin, who has been beside me in nearly every creative endeavor before and after my cancer. She marvelously added the color to these books after so many years and it is a dream come true.

Finally thanks to my family and those close friends who supported me in my artistic and life endeavors and still do.

Table of Contents

1. Acknowledgements - Page 5
2. Chapter 1: I wish I knew - Page 6
3. Chapter 2: I wish I knew how to help - Page 21
4. Chapter 3: I wish I knew who I've become - Page 35
5. About the Author - Page 50

Acknowledgements

I wrote the I wish I knew booklets while struggling to overcome and understand my cancer diagnosis. From every difficult situation comes something amazing, eventually.
These books are my amazing thing, excerpted from my journals where I examined my life situation and sketched my pet finches. Their busy lives inspired me to move forward with my own. Originally three separate booklets for cancer patients, family and friends, I am proud to publish them as a condensed set, in color, with the original illustrations embellished with watercolor overlay.

When I read them, after 15 years, they still move me and let me know that things will be ok, whatever the outcome. I hope they make you feel that way too.

I wish I knew

chapter 1

I wish I knew...sooner

But that is o.k. I thank God I found out when I did. And now that I know, I share the news. Selectively, but I tell people about my cancer. I believe it may encourage others to find out sooner. I share my experiences to give other people courage.

I take care of myself in ways I never did before; resting, expressing my needs, and pampering myself in small and large ways.

Don't beat yourself up.
Pamper yourself and
share your experiences
Try to live well each day.

I wish I knew...
how to ask for help.

It is still hard for me. But it becomes so important as the little things in life become difficult. You will be amazed at how happy people are to do something for you, how they need to help to deal with your situation.

A lot of what I went through is mine, but part of that is all the help I found along the way. Be selective, but ask for help. It will come to you from the most unexpected places.

I wish I knew…
how important good nutrition would be.

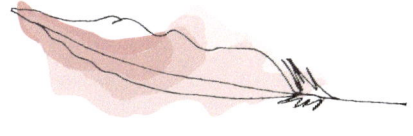

Treatments for cancer are tough on the body, tougher than I had ever imagined. A healthy diet helped me get through them better.

Actually, it went along with the help thing. First I asked people to take me shopping for groceries. Then I asked them to shop for me. Then they started bringing me good food, soups and sauces, fish and fresh fruit. I became good at letting people know what I wanted. It helped us all—I got the food I needed and they felt good about getting me something I could really use.

Things change for a little while. Let go. It is o.k.

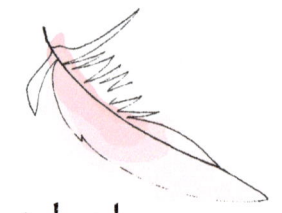

I wish I knew...
      how important rest would be.

I was not a big rest person when I was diagnosed. But I learned how good sleep was for my body and my mind. I made sure I had a good bed and fresh bed linens. I was spending a lot of time there so it became important that it be a comfortable place to be and that I had a special spot for napping or just resting with a cozy blanket.

Sleeping and resting allowed my body to heal. Try to rest as much as you can.

I wish I knew…
 how wonderful people can be.

I am still amazed at the kindness I have been shown while undergoing these treatments. My family and friends have been fantastic. Other wonderful people I met through divine intervention.

People can be abundantly kind—
take advantage of it.

I wish I knew…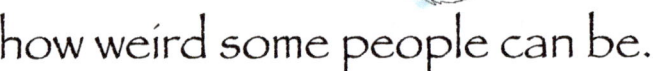
how weird some people can be.

Some people just couldn't, and still can't, handle the fact that I had cancer. They couldn't deal. It was difficult for me too but I learned that stuff was about them, not about me.

It is frightening and it makes it more difficult when people are weird. But you cannot do anything about how other people react. Remember that people do stupid things with loving intentions. It is not a reflection on how wonderful you are or how much they love you.

I wish I knew...
how important my routine would become.

I have always worked out. It connects me to life in a simple way. I worked out most days all through my treatments, from the surgery through chemotherapy and radiation and as I recovered. My routine helped me stay sane. Movement made me feel good so I moved when I could. I adjusted the strength and level of my workouts to what my body told me it could handle.

Remember, you may not be where you were.

You are somewhere new. Find something that feels good, and keep doing it.

I wish I knew...
    how important seeing people for short periods of time would be.

I worked at home through my treatments. While I thanked God for the opportunity, it was isolating. Short visits and conversations were a gift. Laughing offered tremendous relief and crying with someone felt better then crying alone. I was blessed to have family and friends visit, write and call and understand when I couldn't call back.

Let people know when you need them and when you can't handle them. Be candid with yourself and others.

I wish I knew…
    how important keeping the end in mind would become.

Some days the end of my treatments felt very far away and I felt very much alone. Some people plot the end of their treatments on a calendar. I planned a road-trip at the end of mine. People will tell you a million ways to chart your progress but you will know what works for you. The important thing is to mark the milestones and allow people to join you in celebrating them.

Remember that the treatments will end and recovery will begin, sooner than you think.

I wish I knew...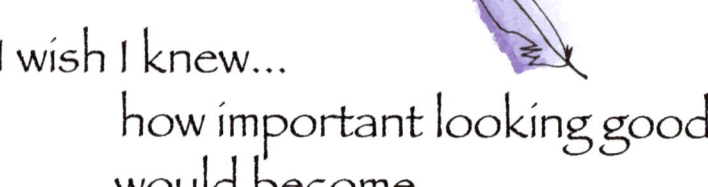
how important looking good would become.

There were so many drastic changes in my body. I had been cut and was still healing when all my hair feel out in a single day. My eyes watered continuously and my nose was always runny.

I had to take my temperature and be careful of infection. There was the heartburn and nausea and constipation and diarrhea. I started not to recognize myself when I looked in the mirror.

It was very helpful for me to dress each day and to dress up when I went out, especially to the doctor's. Looking good buoyed my spirits and helped me feel good around other people. It still does.

I wish I knew...
    how blessed I am.

I never thought I would have breast cancer.
Never. But I live in a world where I can be
diagnosed, treated, and given a second chance;
a chance my mother may not have had and my
grandmother definitely would not have had.
We live in an age of miracles and are truly blessed.

I wish I knew...
 how important my
 spirituality would become.

I stopped going to church years ago, but I never stopped believing in God. The cancer brought me closer to God. Praying became part of every day. Some days it was the best part.

Some days it still is.

If you have faith, be thankful.

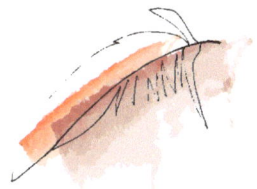

I wish I knew...
     how much love was in my life.

I was separating from my partner of thirteen years when I was diagnosed. I had never felt so alone, but for my pets. I have birds, busy little finches. My drawings of them are here on these pages. Some mornings they were the reason I got out of bed. They couldn't go hungry, so neither could I.

My family and friends made sure to check in on me. When they would visit, it reminded me that there was more to life then treatments. Life holds an abundance of love. Let it encourage you to continue and know that you are important to others.

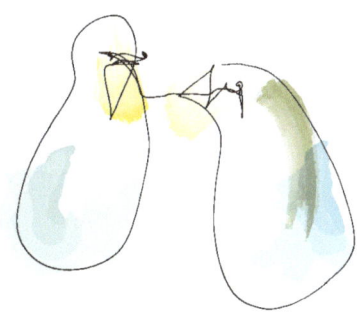

I wish I knew...
how brief this long treatment really was.

It sounded so crazy when the nurse and doctor
told me that this is a brief time in my life.
It seemed to stretch out before me like an eternity.
Now, as I recover and look back on the treatments,
I see how they changed my life in a very short time.
There are things I wish I had done better;
work less, write more, draw more, understand
more. But I made it through in my own way.

I feel more intensely human and aware of myself
now. I have learned about patience and alot
about love. And having made it through these
treatments, I know I can do anything.

The things that I learned are gifts.
They are hard won and precious,
just like you.

I wish I knew how to help

chapter 2

I wish I knew...
   how to tell my friend I am scared.

You don't have to—she is scared enough for both of you. Let her talk about the treatments. Let her tell you how frightened she is. Let her cry if she needs to. Cry with her. She is facing her mortality. Let her vent.

Lots of things are lost with cancer—
feelings of health and control and competence. But lots of things are gained as well. By facing this challenge together, you will both grow.
Your friend will get through this and you will move forward bound together in new ways.

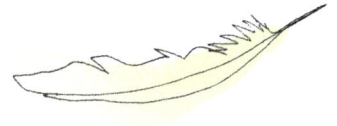

I wish I knew...
how to help my friend with nutrition.

Because her tastes will change from week to week as her body processes the treatments, she will need things she has never needed before. Some of her favorite things may now make her nauseous or give her heartburn. Everyone reacts differently, so her needs will be difficult to predict. You can make her life easier by paying attention to what she needs to deal with the changes. Bring her those things.

I wish I knew...
to knock on my friend's door when going shopping.

If you live in the neighborhood, try to stop by on your way to do your own shopping just to see if you can pick something up for her. Or call and let her know you are going and see if she needs anything. It is so much easier than her calling you to ask for help. A cancer patient is often too tired to cook for herself. Offer to pick up prepared foods like soups and sauces before you visit. When you are cooking, make some extra and bring it over to her. It will be so wonderful for her to have something delicious in the freezer when she is just too tired to make a meal. She will never forget what you provide for her.

I wish I knew...
my friend will need phone calls.

It is hard to gauge because too many calls can be exhausting but when you think of her, call. She can always turn the phone off and it is important for her to know people care, not only during treatments but afterwards. Recovery will take awhile, longer than she or you will want to admit. Stay in contact. Let her know you are there for her. It can make all the difference.

I wish I knew...
little gifts make a big difference.

To know that you are thinking of her when she is so ill will make her feel better. Small gifts like pretty underpants and camisole tops, fragrant candles, scent free soaps and bubble baths, a simple bunch of cut flowers are little things that make a big difference and will remind her you think she is beautiful.

She will need to shop herself for certain things—big plain scarves for her head, hats that are comfortable and pretty, bras that fit well and feel comfortable. If she is up for it, take her shopping to get these things and make it fun. If she can't get out, try to buy her presents that she needs. When you feel ill it is nice to have what you need to make you feel better in even the smallest ways.

I wish I knew...
how tired my friend would be.

Cancer treatments are debilitating. People undergoing the treatments get very tired. Even the smallest tasks can seem insurmountable. Taking out her trash, doing some laundry, or paying for a cleaning person while she is at the doctor's can be a great help. If you can think of ways to make her life a little easier, it will give her more energy to make it through the treatments and take care of herself.

While company can be exhausting, short visits are energizing and will make your friend happy. Visit her as often as you can manage and as often as she allows. And visit on your own. Don't bring kids. They carry lots of love but unfortunately, they also carry too many germs. Have them call or send cards to share their love with her.

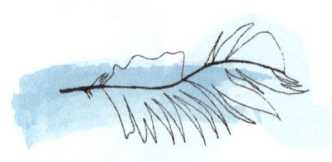

I wish I knew...
to go with my friend to the doctor.

Your friend is processing lots of information. It is a good idea to help her listen to her doctor if she'll let you. She may say she doesn't need you but she does. She may not have told many people about her cancer diagnosis, so if she shares her situation with you, be flattered. Offer to go with her. Say you would like to.

If you can go with her to the surgery, it can help to make it less frightening. Company at the chemotherapy and radiation treatments is also welcome. It can get lonesome and depressing there and it all starts to take over her life. It is nice to have company or at least meet afterwards for a snack. Associating the treatments with meeting a friend and having a good time makes it easier to get through them.

I wish I knew...
   to tell my friend how well
   she is doing.

Recovering from surgery is an ordeal. Making it to all the treatments is an accomplishment. It is often hard to recognize in yourself when you are doing a great job taking care of yourself and beating the cancer. Tell your friend how well she is doing every chance you get. It is important and will help her in ways you cannot imagine.

I wish I knew...
how emotional my friend would get.

A breast cancer patient is going through so much. Your friend will have ups and downs. There are the physical changes, the chemicals in her system, the many changes to her life over which she has no control.

She is frightened and probably angry and depressed. Don't be surprised if she breaks down. Give her a big hug and tell her you love her. Although all your actions will tell her that, she will need to hear it, so say it often.

I wish I knew...
she would need to go out when she felt good.

It may be on short notice. The good days are few and far between when you are undergoing cancer treatments. If the weather is nice, offer to take her to the beach. Bring a quilt and pillow and rest there just watching or listening to the water. If either of you has a fireplace, make a fire and watch the flames. Take her for a drive and a walk in the woods. If she is up for it, take her out to dinner. Just being out in the world can be a comfort. It will help her remember that life is good.

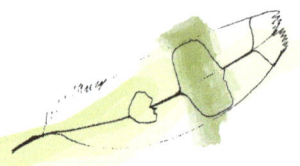

I wish I knew...
the best way to help her cope with hair loss.

If your friend is undergoing chemotherapy it is likely she will lose her hair. Suggest taking her to the hairdresser and cutting her hair short to prepare her for losing it. Emphasize that hair is cosmetic and playful and that the loss is only temporary.

Shopping for stylish wigs while she still has hair and energy is a great idea. Make it fun. If she is feeling well enough, take her to buy big scarves and hats. Help her practice wrapping the scarves on her head so that she will be ready and feel good. She'll need to feel good when she is wearing them. Be honest with her so that she looks as good as she can. It will mean a lot to her.

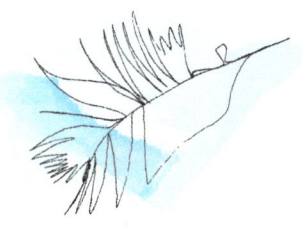

I wish I knew...
    sometimes a joke would heal
    all the pain for awhile.

Laughter really is the best medicine. Share your jokes and your love and try to laugh at life and at yourselves together. Lightening up the situation is almost always the best thing to do, even if it makes you both cry finally. Releasing your emotions is key.

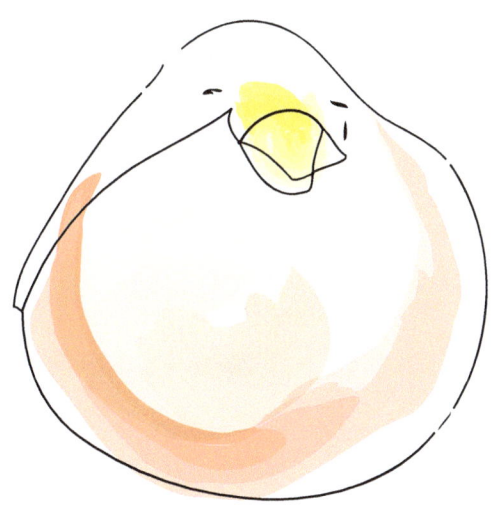

I wish I knew...
    how hard it would be
    to be her friend.

Cancer treatments are tough on the mind and the body. There will be times when your friend is depressed and needy, no matter how together she is. Being there for her won't always be easy, but many times your being there will be the reason she keeps going. That is a gift very few people can give.

Make her laugh. Help her rest. Be there.

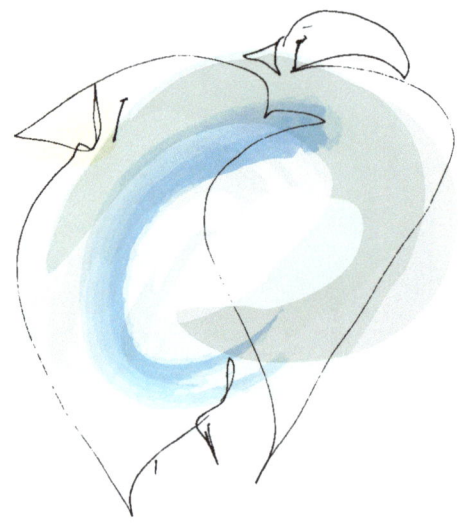

I wish I knew who I've become

chapter 3

REMEMBER

Remember running your fingers across a hairless head.

Remember putting a wig on—really putting a wig on.

Remember being too weak to eat and too weak not to.

Remember crying so hard in your sister's arms
and no one asking why.

Remember reaching deep inside and finding
what you needed to pull yourself through.

Remember the cuts, the burns, the tattoos,
the terror, the pain.

Remember the misunderstanding from friends.

Remember the isolation.

Remember the passages you traveled:
how your trials took you to a higher place.

Remember all the people who cared.

Remember the love: keep it in your heart.

Remember the truth: you made it.

Remember how good you feel now.

                              Remember and live.

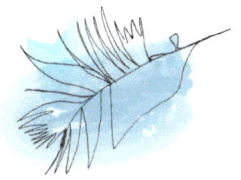

I wish I knew...
who I have become.

But I don't. I am still becoming. That is the gift.

The process isn't over. It is not about the treatments, it is about the journey they engender. You cannot know where it will lead. You can trust. You can experience. You can enjoy. You can know the things you have learned are true. But you cannot know where it all will lead. The end isn't here.
Keep becoming.

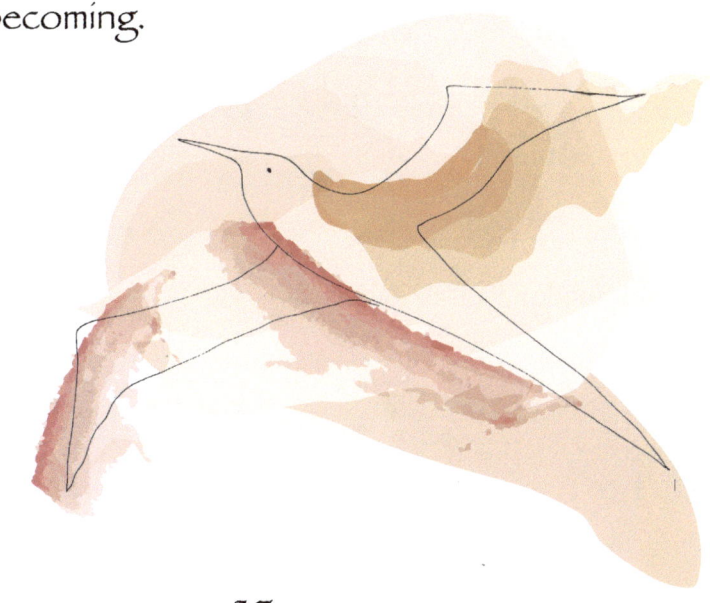

I wish I knew…
I'd become more courageous after my cancer.

I have, very much so. Sometimes, I still feel tired and confused and progress seems slow. I sleep much more than I used to and I dream more, both sleeping and awake. But I am optimistic and working it out: sometimes manically, sometimes with clear direction, but always moving forward.

Because I walked into that chemotherapy room knowing what was in store and because I managed all the radiation treatments without a break, I know I can hold my own with anyone in any room.

Be proud of how far you have come and of the courage you found to get there.

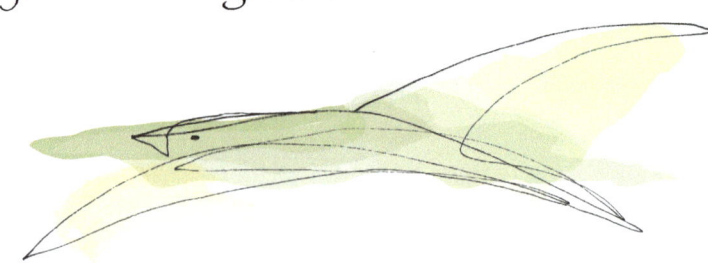

I wish I knew...
I would own the courage I developed.

One day after my hair had grown back in, thick and curly, I cut it really short. I simply felt a need to let go of it. It was so foreign to me. Maybe I was holding onto the patient. Maybe I wanted people to remember what I had been through. Maybe I just wanted to be noticed. I don't really know. But when I cut it, all the curls went too. I couldn't sleep that night. To me, the curls represented changes that I was making in my life because of the cancer. The curls were a visible change. They represented my momentum. When I lost the curls, I was afraid the momentum would go too. That didn't happen. Cosmetic things come and go. But the courage you have gained is permanent.

It is part of you. Relish it.

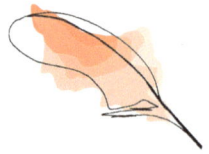

I wish I knew...
this is just the beginning.

So many times I thought it was over: the surgery, the treatments, the resolutions, the changes. But it is not over.

As I learn to take more risks, as I learn to trust myself, as I listen to the person I held back for so long, I know that I have started an entirely new chapter in my life. I am just where I am supposed to be and I am exactly who I am supposed to be.

Trust that you will find your stride.

It is all just beginning.

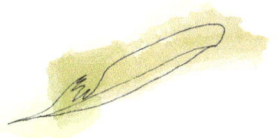

I wish I knew...
to embrace being a survivor more.

I am learning. Other women who have had breast cancer have been very helpful. Other cancer survivors took great care of me during treatment. I love them all for it.

But just being a survivor? I resist that label. Surviving is the starting point but I want more.

I am determined to thrive. The distinction means a lot. As I move through the transitions that surviving brings, I am determined to dream my dreams and discover how to make them reality.

By thriving you help others who have survived.

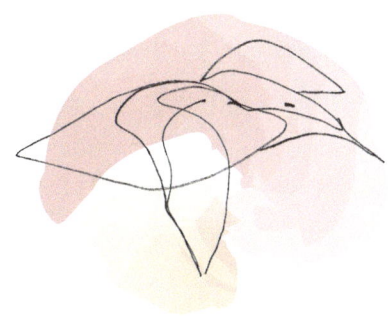

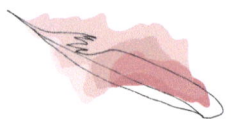

I wish I knew...
how to explain to people that I have changed.

I stumble. I hesitate. I speak out of turn. I lash out. Sometimes I don't recognize myself. Sometimes, when I do, I wish I could go back to the person I was. I knew her so well.

It is ok. Tell yourself that. If people can't handle who you have become or what you have to say, that is about them, not about you. Be who you are. Let go of your need for others to approve of your life.

Embrace the new person you have become.

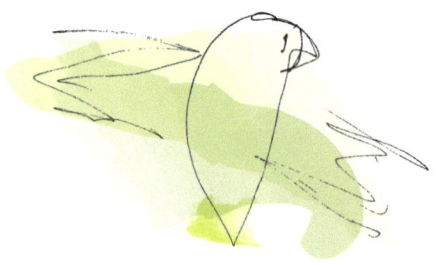

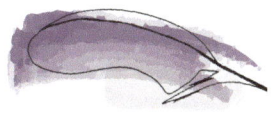

I wish I knew...
I would become better at defining what I want.

It takes practice, but you need to know what you want. People have so many ideas to help you. They have so many opinions on what you should do. Many of them come from a place of love. Listen to them, certainly. But analyze them. Be comfortable saying no. Practice it.

You can only do so much.

Make sure that you do what is right for you.

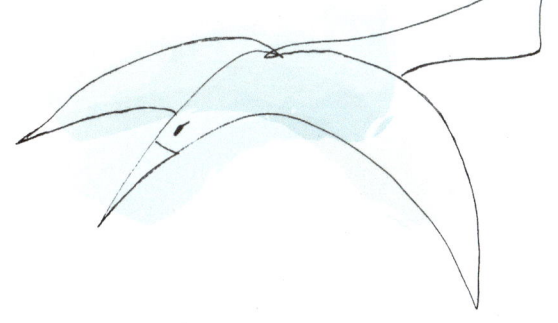

I wish I knew...
to stay open to re-evaluating my life's work.

Cancer made me see that the choices we make become our lives. I had never been very happy with my work before my diagnosis, but I was very good at it. Some would say excellent. So at first I continued to strive to be even better at it rather than trying to see how I could be happier.

The only thing harder than leaving my job of eighteen years would have been to stay, to block out who I had become and deny that I needed a change to be happy.

Ask yourself how and where you want to spend the rest of your life. Be open to the answer you find within.

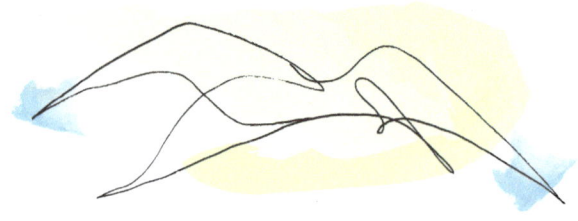

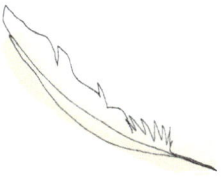

I wish I knew...
to nurture the parts of me I had neglected.

Writing every day while undergoing treatment helped me understand what I was going through. Drawing made me smile. Working out empowered me. Seeing friends and family let me know I was loved. The things that I thought could wait for weekends or lunch hours were the things that served me best in my life or death situation.

Most of us have special things that we put off for "the right time." Now is the right time.

Pursue the things you love. Every second, every moment, every day counts.

I wish I knew...
that my primary relationship of the heart might not fit with the person I have become.

It is painful to admit that someone you have traveled with so far cannot explore your new world. But it is more damaging to stay in a place you've outgrown.

Some ties may grow stronger. Some may fade. Most will change, as you have changed. Develop a new relationship with yourself. Plot your course and move forward.

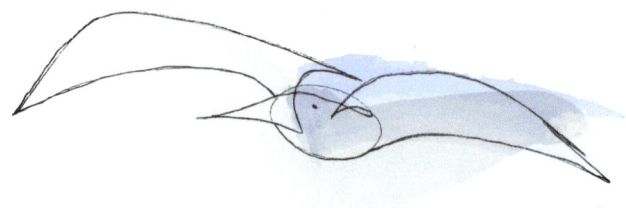

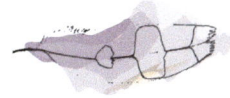

I wish I knew...
I had learned the lessons I needed.

I have learned a lot. More than I ever imagined I could. More than I ever wanted to. Through the shock and the sorrow and the many poignant moments, I have learned about myself, about life and so much about love. I have learned not to judge and to take each moment as a gift.

Breathe deeply. The lessons will not be easy but they will move you along your path.

Allow things to happen. Learn.

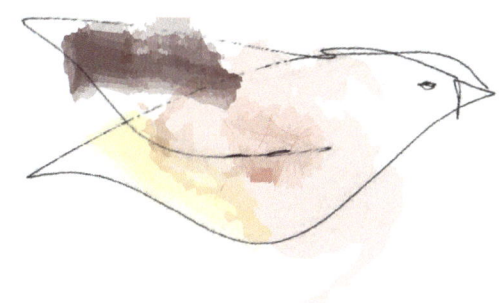

I wish I knew...
how good I would feel again.

Some days, even long after the treatments, I still feel so badly: tired, depressed, achy. But some days I feel good again and it is such a nice surprise.

After the resting, after the self-examination, after all the tears and all the sorrow, after all the love and the hurt, the healing happens. The sun will come out and touch your face and you will feel joy and happiness and you will know in your heart that life is good. You will feel energetic, true and sure. Better and stronger and more positive than ever. Maybe not everyday. Maybe not right away, but soon.

Hold onto that. Count on it.

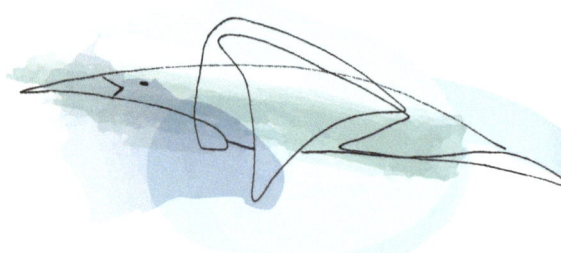

I wish I knew...
you make your own happy endings.

Once, when I was really sick, I asked my mother where my happy ending was. Why couldn't I have what other people have? I felt so very bad. My future lay before me like a chore, like a curse. But now, after all this effort and pain, I believe I can make my own happy endings if I persevere and trust. When it is time, life will cooperate and it will all come together.

You are a survivor. You made it.
Dream and work toward your dream.
Be like the birds on these pages. Fly.

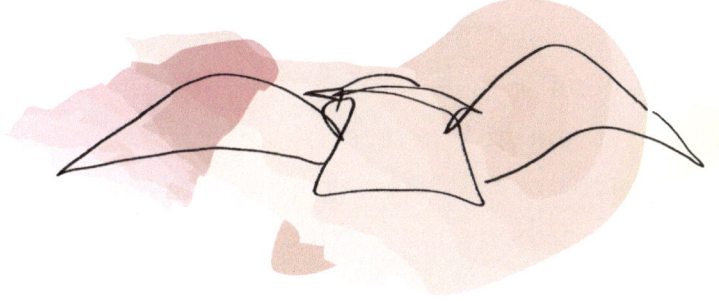

About the Author

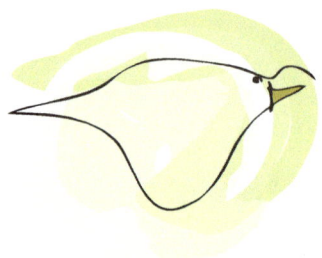

Fanny Barry is an entrepreneur, artist and yogi who lives in Tulum Mexico by way of Boston, Massachusetts. She wrote these poetic observations on the cancer experience while undergoing and recovering from treatment. Part of that recovery included starting her life over on a small jungle plot across the street from the incredible and at that time unknown and unpopulated Tulum Beach. She recently published her memoir called *Map of Life and Beauty* which talks about that incredible recovery journey.

She blogs at www.thatbarrygirl.com. She built a yoga studio called Tribal in 2015 which she manages and teaches alongside several other talented yogis. Tribal hosts guests in personal yoga retreats, many of which have been cancer survivors. She is working on a children's book and a series based on Map of Life and Beauty. After 15 years cancer free, Joanne Fanny Barry is truly thriving not just surviving.

www.ingramcontent.com/pod-product-compliance
Lightning Source LLC
Chambersburg PA
CBHW042311150426
43198CB00006B/117